Sublime Imagination

ANTI-STRESS COLOURING BOOK

Images by Dream State Studio

Photo Credits

All illustrations are reworkings of images drawn
from Dream State Studio/123RF,
except the image of page 48 by Volodymyr Karpenyuk/123RF.

Graphic Design

Paola Piacco

WS White Star Publishers® is a registered trademark
property of White Star s.r.l.

© 2016 White Star s.r.l.
Piazzale Luigi Cadorna, 6
20123 Milan, Italy
www.whitestar.it

Translation: ICEIGEO, Milan

All rights reserved. No part of this publication may be reproduced,
stored in a retrieval system or transmitted in any form or by
any means, electronic, mechanical, photocopying, recording
or otherwise, without written permission from the publisher.

ISBN 978-88-544-1089-3
1 2 3 4 5 6   20 19 18 17 16

Printed in China

Sublime Imagination

ANTI-STRESS COLOURING BOOK

WHITE STAR PUBLISHERS

Introduction

Imagine finding yourself inside a dream, made up of shapes, lines, figures, animals, wonderful butterflies, lush plants . . . Just as in a dream, you will fell immersed in a dimension in which reality and imagination are intertwined, without being able to distinguish clearly whether what you are observing is what you think you are seeing. In this case, however, you need not close your eyes; rather, you must keep them wide open! Because the web of this dreamlike vision takes life, stretching on the pages of this colouring book illustration after illustration. The marvellous illustrations of this book came to life first in the fervid creative imagination of the team from Dream State Studio, a Taiwanese agency of illustrators with elegant stroke. When you look at their drawings, you will marvel at the very fine details making up the images: every detail has already in itself a particular aesthetic taste, thus their combination forms an even more amazing general design. A butterfly with outstretched wings holds within it the shapes of two facing lions, but also the lions are in their turn made up of smaller parts: flowers, leaves, plant parts . . . Everything is interpenetrated, transformed, mixed, to form new suggestions and creative ideas. The seahorse observes his 'namesake' with four legs, a peacock spreads its marvellous tail which seems to recall the form of an Indian mandala, a great round flower becomes the shell of a crawling snail . . . let yourselves be involved, astonished, transported, fascinated and conquered by this magical world. And, above all, let yourselves be inspired: because you have the task of completing these splendid illustrations, filling them with colours. Give full rein to your imagination. Take up coloured pencils or marker pens and give vibrant colours or more delicate shades to the details of the illustrations. You create, too, according to your taste, a fantastic, unique and kaleidoscopic world. Learn to concentrate while relaxing, and you will discover a pastime that can keep you busy and will provide you with hours of fun and well-being. You cannot always remember dreams when you awake. In contrast, at the end of this journey among the colours, you will have a tangible memory to admire and to show with pride.